CREATIVE
CHRISTMAS TREE
DECORATIONS

CREATIVE
CHRISTMAS TREE
DECORATIONS

Over 30 inspiring projects for decorating your
Christmas tree with innovative eye-catching ornaments

CAROLYN BELL

LORENZ BOOKS

Lorenz Books is an imprint of Anness Publishing Limited
Blaby Road, Wigston, Leicestershire LE18 4SE
info@anness.com
www.lorenzbooks.com; www.annesspublishing.com

If you like the images in this book and would like to investigate using them for publishing, promotions or advertising,
please visit our website www.practicalpictures.com for more information.

A CIP catalogue record for this book is available from the British Library

Publisher: Joanna Lorenz
Senior Editor: Catherine Barry
Designer: Simon Wilder

Measurements
Both imperial and metric measurements have been given in the text.
Where conversions produce an awkward number, these have been rounded for convenience
but will produce an accurate result if one system is used throughout.

PUBLISHER'S NOTE
Although the advice and information in this book are believed to be accurate and true at the time of going to press,
neither the authors nor the publisher can accept any legal responsibility or liability for any errors or omissions
that may have been made nor for any inaccuracies nor for any loss, harm or injury that comes about
from following instructions or advice in this book.

ACKNOWLEDGEMENTS
The publishers would like to thank the following craftspeople: Fiona Barnett p 26; Petra Boase p56; Penny Boylan pp 14, 20,
28, 30, 42, 43, 46, 52; Louise Brownlow p 36; Annabel Crutchley p 32; Marion Elliot p 54; Joanna Farrow p 24; Stephanie Harvey
p 22; Christine Kingdom p 12; Mary Maguire pp 16, 40; Gloria Nicol pp 8, 48; Cheryl Owen p 58; Theresa Pateman p 34;
Deborah Schneebeli Morrell p 18; Isabel Stanley pp 10, 15; Liz Wagstaff p 60; Pamela Westland pp 23, 38, 39; Ann Zwemmer p 50.
Thanks also to the following photographers:
Steve Dalton pp 34, 40; Michelle Garrett pp 20, 24, 30, 52; Nelson Hargreaves pp 23, 38, 39; Janine Hosegood pp 14, 28, 42, 43, 46;
Tim Imrie p 32; Gloria Nicol p 36; Debbie Patterson pp 26, 54, 60; Graham Rae p 50; Heine Schneebeli p 18; Steve Tanner p 58;
Peter Williams pp 8, 10, 12, 15, 16, 22, 48; Polly Wreford p56.
All photographs © Anness Publishing Limited.

CONTENTS

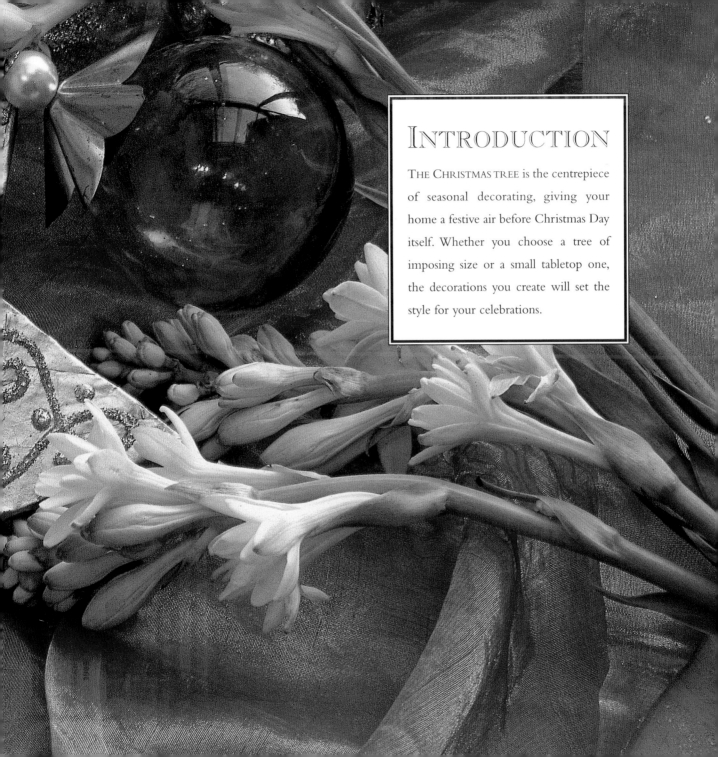

INTRODUCTION

THE CHRISTMAS TREE is the centrepiece of seasonal decorating, giving your home a festive air before Christmas Day itself. Whether you choose a tree of imposing size or a small tabletop one, the decorations you create will set the style for your celebrations.

SHINY SNOWFLAKES

These sparkling decorations are easy to make by simply cutting patterns out of shiny reflective papers.
A mixture of gold, silver and coloured papers will reflect the tree lights perfectly.

YOU WILL NEED
pencil
pair of compasses (compass)
reflective papers in gold, silver and
several colours
scissors
tracing paper
craft knife
cutting mat
gold thread

1 Draw a circle on the back of the reflective paper and cut it out. Fold the circle in half three times. Photocopy the patterns from the back of the book, enlarging if necessary.

2 Trace one of the geometric designs on to a pattern and transfer it on to the folded shiny paper circle. Use a sharp pencil as the detail is intricate and must be precise.

3 Cut out the traced pattern shapes, using a craft knife to make small, internal cuts. Unfold the circle and flatten. Do the same with the other papers and geometric patterns.

4 For the curved pattern, unfold once and fold in half the other way, then cut out triangular notches along the fold line. Attach lengths of gold thread to hang the snowflakes.

SEQUINNED BALLS

Sequins make wonderful Christmas tree decorations, twinkling and sparkling in the light.
You can follow this design or create your own patterns.

YOU WILL NEED
marker pen
compressed cotton spheres
(styrofoam balls)
concave sequins in a variety
of colours and shapes
lill (straight) pins
beading thread
beading needle
small bronze-coloured glass beads
fluted metal beads
dressmaker's pins

1 Use a marker pen to divide each cotton sphere into quarters. Mark around the middle of the sphere to divide it into eight sections.

2 Outline the sections with sequins in different colours, attaching them with lill pins. Overlap the sequins slightly so that the cotton sphere does not show through.

3 Fill in each section with sequins, again overlapping the sequins slightly to hide the sphere. You may want to make each section a different colour, or mix colours together.

4 Make a loop for hanging and thread small bronze-coloured beads on to it. Thread a metal bead on to a dressmaker's pin and press into the sphere to secure the loop.

Ribbon Ornaments

A welcome change from shop-bought decorations, these stylish designs make use of the many attractive ribbons now available. Silk ribbon is the most appealing as it will catch the light.

You will need
RIBBON BALL
polystyrene (styrofoam) ball
assortment of plain ribbons
dressmaker's pins
scissors
patterned ribbon
gold lace pins
small gold beads
gold coin pendants
large, ornate gold bead

CONE PARCEL
narrow ribbon
pine cone
wide ribbon or ready-made bow
all-purpose glue

GOLDEN TASSEL
small compressed cotton
(styrofoam) ball
scissors
gold ribbon
all-purpose glue
needle

RIBBON BALL

1 Cover the ball completely with a variety of ribbons, securing to the ball with pins. Decorate the ball with gold beads and coin pendants.

GOLDEN TASSEL

1 Make a hole through the ball and insert lengths of ribbon. Dab glue on to the ball, then fold down the ribbons until the ball is covered.

CONE PARCEL

1 Wrap narrow ribbon around the cone as if wrapping a parcel. Tie a bow at the top and dab with glue to secure. Make a ribbon loop to hang.

2 Wrap a ribbon around the base. To make a loop, thread the needle with a ribbon and insert through the hole in the ball. Knot the ends and trim.

RAFFIA BALLS

For a natural alternative to glitzy glass ornaments, hang up these little balls covered with raffia.

Raffia balls make a splendid display hung alongside a garland of deep red hearts suspended between a length of natural twine.

YOU WILL NEED
fine copper wire
scissors
small polystyrene (styrofoam) balls
double-sided tape
natural (garden) raffia

1 Shape a piece of wire into a loop and stick the ends into the ball. Cover the ball completely with tape. Holding a short strand at the top of the ball, wind the raffia around the ball, working from top to bottom.

2 When you have covered the ball, remove the wire loop. Tie the end of the raffia to the length you left free at the beginning. Using a few lengths of raffia, form a loop for hanging.

Glittery Balls

Dress up plain gold and silver shop-bought balls with delicate patterns traced in glitter.

1 Squeeze contour paste on to the balls in zigzags. Pour glitter over the contour paste, working in sections and allowing each section to dry. Rest the ball on a roll of tape or in an old glass while it dries.

2 If you want to add some more intricate detail to the ball, allow all the glitter sections to dry before adding more dabs of contour paste and sprinkling with glitter.

A variety of glitter and gilded balls make a perfect Christmas gift, arranged in a plain box, lined with gold and silver paper.

WIRE ANGEL

This elegant Christmas angel will grace the top of your tree year after year.

YOU WILL NEED
silver- or gold-plated wire,
1 mm (0.039 in) thick
round-nosed pliers
parallel pliers
wire cutters
narrow ribbon
silver or gold star

1 Use the template at the back of the book as a guide. Leaving 5 cm (2 in) at the end, begin to bend the wire around the template. Use round-nosed pliers for the larger curls and parallel pliers for the more delicate curls.

2 Continue bending the wire into the angel shape. When you reach the waist, bend the wire across to form the waistband. Make a series of seven long horizontal loops with curled ends back along the waistband.

3 When you reach the final curls of the shoulder, loop the wire around the back of the shoulder and under the bottom of the wing. Finish off with a coil, then cut off the wire.

4 Using the wire left at the start, bind the shoulder and wing together. Cut off the end. Thread ribbon through the loops in the waistband and hang a star from the hand.

HARLEQUIN EGGS

These rich metallic-effect ornaments are in fact blown eggs, decorated with gold and silver gilt cream. Suspend them from the Christmas tree or an alternative such as pussy willow or holly.

YOU WILL NEED
hen's eggs
pale blue acrylic paint
flat artist's paintbrush
white pencil
fine paintbrush
gilt cream in gold and silver
soft cloth
wire egg-holders

Plain gold gilded eggs are also very decorative. They are blown first, then gilded with gilt cream and polished to a shine. A combination of silver and gold eggs, suspended from the branches of a real Christmas tree, will look extremely elegant.

1 Blow the eggs by making a hole at either end and blowing the contents out. Paint half of each egg with pale blue. Leave to dry, then paint the other half in the same colour.

2 Using a white pencil, and with a steady hand, draw horizontal and vertical lines over the egg to make a checked pattern. This pattern can be adjusted to suit your own design.

3 Using a fine paintbrush, paint gold gilt cream in alternate squares, taking care to keep the edges neat. Leave to dry. Paint the silver squares in the same way and leave to dry.

4 Carefully polish the egg with a soft cloth to a high shine. Hold the two prongs of the wire egg-holder firmly together and push them into the hole at the top of the egg for hanging.

GILDED STARS

Hang these festive stars on different lengths of ribbon for a sparkling effect.

You will need
tracing paper
pencil
squares of MDF (medium density
fiberboard), 15 x 15 cm (6 x 6 in)
black marker pen
coping saw or fretsaw
sandpaper
electric or hand drill
red oxide spray primer
water-based size
2.5 cm (1 in) wide decorator's
paintbrush
Dutch metal leaf in gold and aluminium
burnishing brush or soft cloth
wire (steel) wool
methylated spirit (turpentine)
shellac varnish
acrylic varnishing wax
acrylic paints in green and blue
containers for mixing paint
soft cloths
all-purpose glue
dome-shaped plastic jewels
ribbon

1 Trace the template from the back of the book and transfer it on to MDF. Cut out stars with a saw, sandpaper the edges and drill a hole at the top. Spray both sides with primer.

2 Paint on a thin, even coat of size and leave for 20-30 minutes. Gild each star with gold or aluminium metal leaf, then burnish with a burnishing brush or soft cloth.

3 Dip some wire wool into a little methylated spirit and gently rub the edges of each star. Paint a thin, even coat of shellac varnish over the gold leaf and varnishing wax over the aluminium leaf.

4 Mix the green and blue paints with a little water. Paint each star, leave for 5 minutes, then remove most of the paint with a cloth. Glue a plastic jewel in the centre. Tie a piece of ribbon through the hole for hanging.

PRECIOUS SHELLS

Nature's intricate decoration is often hard to beat, but at Christmas time we can enhance it with subtle gilding. These charming shells can either be hung individually or strung together to form a garland.

Shells of all shapes and sizes can be gilded in this way; more intricately shaped shells look particularly pleasing. If you are using shells you have collected yourself from the seashore, make sure that they are scrupulously clean and free from sand before you begin gilding.

YOU WILL NEED
shells
blue emulsion paint
two 1 cm (½ in) wide decorator's
paintbrushes
water-based gold size
Dutch metal leaf in aluminium or
gold on transfer paper
pale shellac varnish
strong glue
ribbon

1 Paint each shell with two coats of blue paint. Allow to dry. Paint size on to the shells, smoothing out any air bubbles with the brush. Leave to dry until the size becomes clear.

2 Press the metal sheets on to the shells and use a brush to remove any excess. Varnish and leave to dry. Dab glue on to the tip of each shell and attach a ribbon for hanging.

GILDED DETAILS

One of the quickest and easiest ways to create a gilded Christmas ornament is with gold or silver spray paint.
Here are some simple ideas.

Glue nuts together in clusters, either keeping the same variety together or mixing interesting shaped nuts. When the glue has set firm, push a stub wire (floral pin) through a gap between the nuts, twist it to make a loop and tie on a decorative ribbon or bow.

Be bold in your choice of subjects to spray: dried mushrooms or toadstools are an unusual choice. Dry the fungi in an airing cupboard or an oven at the lowest setting with the door slightly open. After spraying, tie them singly, in pairs or in groups with colourful ribbons.

Store-bought biscuits in fun shapes can be sprayed gold and they make wonderful subjects for the enthusiastic gilder. You can buy edible gold spray from specialist cake decorating outlets.

Fruit of all shapes and sizes – pears in particular –
look opulent spatter-sprayed with gold or silver paint.
Fix a hook to each stalk and tie on a shiny bow to
attach to the tree.

GINGERBREAD PLAQUES

These pretty edible decorations use a ready-made gingerbread mix and will be popular with all ages.

YOU WILL NEED
two large baking sheets
one quantity (batch) golden gingerbread dough
rolling pin
8 cm (3¼ in) gingerbread man biscuit (cookie) cutter
skewer
wire rack
one quantity (batch) royal icing
piping bag, fitted with writing nozzle
two bowls
food colouring in green and blue
lemon juice
silver dragees
narrow gingham ribbon

There are a whole range of biscuit and pastry cutters available on the market. Santas are a traditional family favourite.

1 Preheat the oven to 180°C/ 350°F/Gas 4. Grease the baking sheets. Roll out the gingerbread dough on a floured surface and cut out the gingerbread figures. Space them well apart on the baking sheets.

2 Re-roll the dough trimmings and cut into strips, 1 cm (½ in) wide and 28 cm (11 cm) long. Place a strip around each man. Make a hole in the top with a skewer. Bake for 12-15 minutes, then cool on a wire rack.

3 Put icing in the piping bag. Pipe in the details. Divide the remaining icing equally into two bowls. Colour one green and the other blue. Thin the icing with lemon juice.

4 Ice the body of each figure. Add a row of dragee buttons. Leave to set for two hours. Decorate the edges and buttons with white icing. Thread the biscuits with ribbon for hanging.

Fruit and Flower Decorations

Natural decorations complement an evergreen tree perfectly.

You will need
Floral Stars and Trees
knife
block of florist's foam
pastry (cookie) cutters in star and
Christmas tree shapes
loose, dried lavender
gold dust powder
plastic bag, with no holes
florist's adhesive
loose, dried tulip and rose petals
(optional)
cranberries (optional)
gold cord
scissors

Dried Fruit Decorations
gold cord
dried oranges and limes
florist's adhesive
dried red and yellow rose heads
cinnamon sticks

Floral Stars and Trees

1 Cut the block of foam into approximately 2.5 cm (1 in) thick slices. Using the pastry cutters, press out star and tree shapes. Put the lavender with two tablespoons of gold dust powder in the plastic bag and shake to mix. Liberally coat all the surfaces of the foam shapes with florist's adhesive.

2 Place the shapes in the plastic bag and shake. As a variation, press dried tulip and rose petals on to the shapes before putting them in the bag; only the exposed glued areas will pick up the lavender. Alternatively glue a cranberry to the centre of the stars. Make a small hole in each shape, and thread with gold cord for hanging.

Dried Fruit Decorations

1 Tie gold cord around the fruit, and knot it on top to form a hanging loop. Stick a rose head to the top next to the knotted cord. Dab glue on to cinnamon sticks and place them next to the rose head.

Winter Heart

A plump, soft heart edged in bold blanket stitch will make an original addition to your tree.

1 Trace the template at the back of the book and cut out two hearts, in each fabric. Cut two small strips for the cross. Use the template again to cut out a piece of wadding, then trim off 1 cm (½ in) all around the edge.

2 Pin the cross pieces on to the contrasting fabric and attach with large stitches, using three strands of embroidery thread.

3 Pin all the layers together, sandwiching the wadding between the fabric hearts. Make a loop of twine for hanging the ornament and insert the ends in the top.

4 Sew all around the edges of the heart in blanket stitch using three strands of embroidery thread. Make sure the hanging loop is secured with the stitches.

Rococo Star

Persuade the fairy to take a well-earned rest this year, and make a magnificent gold star to take pride of place at the top of the tree or hanging from the branches.

YOU WILL NEED
tracing paper
pencil
thin cardboard or paper
scissors
corrugated cardboard
craft knife
cutting mat
newspaper
PVA (white) glue
large decorator's paintbrush
container for glue
gold spray paint
gold relief paint
gold glitter
gold braid (optional)

1 Trace the template from the back of the book and transfer it on to cardboard or paper. Cut out and draw around it on the corrugated cardboard, using a craft knife and cutting mat. Tear the newspaper into small strips and brush watered-down glue on to both sides. Stick the newspaper strips on to the star.

2 Neatly cover the edges and points of the star with the newpaper strips. Allow to dry, then apply a second layer. If the star begins to buckle, place it under a heavy weight. When completely dry, spray both sides with gold paint and let dry.

3 Draw a design on one side in gold relief paint and sprinkle with glitter while wet. Allow to dry completely before repeating the design on the other side. If you are hanging the star, attach gold braid from the top point with a dab of glue.

ELEGANT TASSELS

These delicate tassels make stunning Christmas ornaments suspended from the branches of the tree.

YOU WILL NEED
scissors
silk or metallic embroidery threads
(floss)
thin polyester thread
cord
comb
fine twine

1 Cut and fold lengths of embroidery threads and place them on top of the polyester thread. Loop a length of cord, knot the ends and place on the embroidery threads. Tie the polyester thread tightly around the cord.

2 Cut through the folded ends of the embroidery threads, then comb out the tassel. Make a small loop with the fine twine.

Tassels look especially splendid when gilded. These tassels have been coated with red oxide primer, left to dry and then sprayed with three applications of gold spray paint. The fronds of the tassels may form clumps which can be eliminated with a comb before they dry.

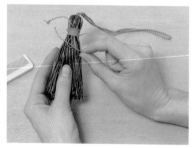

3 Working from top to bottom of the ball of the tassel, neatly bind the twine tightly around the top of the tassel as shown. Pass the end of the twine through the loop.

4 Pull the twine up into the binding and snip off the ends. Make a loop in a strand of the cord and pass the cord through the loop. Trim the cut ends of the tassel and hang from the cord.

HANGING JUGGLERS

This inventive decoration is made from a wire coathanger and small pieces of polymer clay.

YOU WILL NEED
pliers
wire coathanger
gold aerosol paint
epoxy resin glue
¼ block modelling polymer clay
earring wires with loops
modelling tools
pastry (cookie) cutters
sandpaper
thick needle
acrylic paints in bright colours
fine artist's paintbrushes
varnish
nylon fishing line
shell-shaped jewellery findings
gold cord for hanging

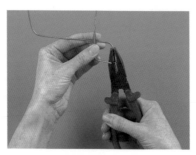

1 Cut the hook and twisted section off the hanger. Twist half the remaining wire into a double-diamond-shaped frame. Spray with gold paint, then glue the wires where they cross.

2 Mould four thumbnail-sized pieces of clay into egg shapes for the heads of the figures. Trim an earring wire, form a hook in the end and embed into each head.

3 Roll small pieces of clay for the limbs and an oblong for each torso. Assemble the bodies and smooth any seams with sandpaper. Cut five stars, two a little larger. Roll five bead shapes and pierce. Bake, as instructed.

4 Paint the figures, beads and stars, then varnish. Assemble the figures and stars on the frame using fishing line and findings. Tie cord to the top for hanging, then glue the large stars on either side, sandwiching the wire.

Embroidered Dragonflies

These charming ornaments will make very original decorations for your tree.

You will need
tracing paper
pencil
black marker pen
water-soluble fabric
embroidery hoop
opalescent cellophane
small pieces of sheer synthetic organdie
in brown and green
dressmaker's pins
sewing machine with fine needle
metallic thread in two thicknesses
spray varnish
scissors
glittery pipecleaners
sewing needle
small glass beads
fine wire
all-purpose glue

1 Trace the templates on to stretched fabric. Put the cellophane between two pieces of organdie and pin under the hoop. Stitch around the wings in straight stitch using metallic thread.

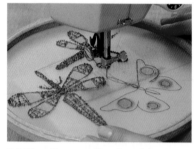

2 Using fine metallic thread in the needle and thick thread in the bobbin, sew the outlines in straight stitch. Fill in the shapes. Remove the hoop and dissolve the fabric in water.

3 Varnish the insects and leave to dry. Cut a pipecleaner longer than each body and sew to the underside as far as the head. Trim and bend the rest of the embroidery under the head and body to cover the pipecleaner.

4 Fold the wings into a raised position and stitch. Thread glass beads on to the wire, twist into antennae and attach to the head. Glue the insects directly to the branches of the tree.

FRUIT AND SPICE ORNAMENTS

This selection of simple ideas adds a splash of colour and a delightful, fresh scent to the tree.

Tie decorative bundles of cinnamon sticks together with ribbon for a sweetly scented tree trim. Secure cranberries to the ribbon with an all-purpose glue; this will complement the bright garlands of cranberries threaded on to sewing thread which also adorn the tree.

Thick, shiny orange rings look good enough to eat, even when they have been dried. Cut 6 mm (¼ in) slices from a large orange, place on a rack and dry in an oven at a low temperature for about one hour. Push a knife through just below the peel and thread with a ribbon.

Deck the tree with the prettiest of citrus fruits, tiny egg-shaped kumquats, by threading them on to medium stub wires. Loop the circlets over the tree branches or tie them with complementary or contrasting ribbon. You could also use satsumas, tangerines or clementines.

These unusual ornaments are made by sticking a small white cake candle to the base of a white curtain ring. Cut a piece of gold sequin trim to fit the curtain ring and stick it on the back of the ring. Add a gold-sprayed star anise seedpod at the front for extra glitz.

CLASSIC POMANDERS

Pomanders have been a favourite Christmas decoration since Elizabethan times.

YOU WILL NEED
navel or thin-skinned oranges
cloves
masking tape
large paperclip
ribbon

1 Stud the fruit with cloves. The traditional design is made by wrapping masking tape around the fruit in a criss cross fashion to divide it into four equal sections. The tape is then outlined with cloves.

2 Push the loop of a large paperclip deep into the top of the fruit to make a loop to hang the ribbon. For a dry-look pomander, keep the fruit in a warm cupboard for 1–2 weeks before hanging.

There are many interesting classic pomander desgins based on geometric patterns, such as circles, squares and stars. The pomanders shown above were slashed vertically with a knife in a design reminiscent of a Renaissance doublet. The fruit was then dried on foil in an oven on a very low heat overnight to create a deep colour and a crisp texture. Dried pomanders should last at least 6–8 weeks.

Festive Figures

Polymer clay is perfect for making Christmas ornaments as it is easy to use and extremely versatile.

YOU WILL NEED
roller
polymer clay in various colours
Christmas pastry (cookie) cutters
modelling tool
fine artist's paintbrush
plastic straw
bronze powders in various colours
varnish
glue
rhinestones
cocktail stick (toothpick)
narrow ribbon

1 Roll out the clay to a thickness of 1 cm (½ in) and press out the shapes using pastry cutters. Cut a good selection of figures and sizes.

2 Draw markings with a modelling tool and make small indentations for the rhinestones on the reindeer with the blunt end of a paintbrush.

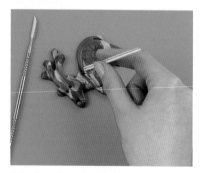

3 Make a hanging hole in the top centre with a straw. Brush on different coloured bronze powders and blend together. Bake following the manufacturer's instructions.

4 Apply a coat of varnish and leave to dry. Glue rhinestones in the indentations, using a cocktail stick. Thread a length of ribbon through the hole for hanging.

GILDED GLASS SPHERES

Transform plain balls into unique ornaments. Simple motifs such as circles, triangles and stars work best.

YOU WILL NEED
plain round glass balls
detergent
white spirit (paint thinner)
gold glass (relief) outliner
kitchen paper
jam jar
wire-edged or other wide ribbon
scissors

Simple, bold shapes will look best on small balls. Take your inspiration from stained glass windows in churches, mixing geometric shapes with elegant curves or curlicues.

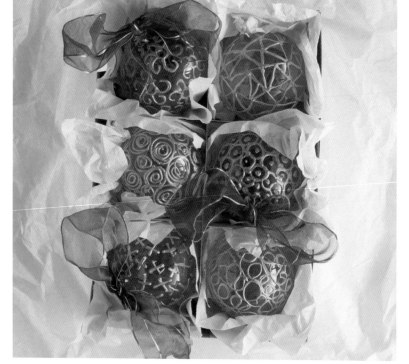

1 Clean the balls carefully with detergent and white spirit. Working on one side, squeeze the outliner on to the glass. Wipe any mistakes with kitchen paper before they dry.

2 Rest the ball in an empty jam jar and leave for 24 hours to dry thoroughly. Decorate the other side and leave to dry again. Thread a length of ribbon through the top of the ornament and tie in a bow.

BUTTON GARLAND

A collection of buttons takes on a new life as an unusual garland for the Christmas tree.

YOU WILL NEED
assortment of buttons in
various sizes and colours
glue gun
glue sticks
garden twine
scissors

The muted colours of the button garland look particularly effective when hung alongside the rich tones of gingerbread hearts and stars.

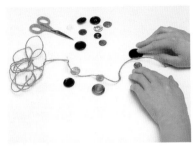

1 Spread all the buttons out so that you can choose a variety of colours and sizes. Balance the weight of the buttons by spacing small ones with larger ones along the garland.

2 Put a small dab of glue on the back of a button. Lay the twine on top and wait until the glue hardens. Glue all the buttons along the twine in the same way, spacing them evenly. Tie around the tree.

Edible Ornaments

These tasty ornaments will delight both children and adults. This recipe makes approximately 12 ornaments.

YOU WILL NEED
baking sheet
non-stick baking paper (parchment)
175 g/6 oz/1½ cups plain flour
75 g/3 oz/5 tbsp butter
40 g/1½ oz/3 tbsp caster
(superfine) sugar
egg white
30 ml/2 tbsp orange juice
rolling pin
Christmas tree pastry (cookie) cutter
round 1 cm (½ in) pastry
(cookie) cutter
225 g/8 oz coloured fruit sweets
(candies)
wire rack
coloured ribbons

1 Preheat the oven to 180°C/350°F/ Gas 4. Line a baking sheet with baking paper. Sift the flour into a mixing bowl. Cut the butter into pieces and rub into the flour until it resembles breadcrumbs. Stir in the sugar, egg white and enough orange juice to form a soft dough. Knead on a lightly floured surface until smooth.

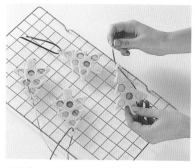

2 Roll out thinly and stamp out as many shapes as possible using a Christmas tree cutter. Transfer the shapes to the lined baking sheet spaced well apart. Using the round cutter, stamp out six circles from each tree. Cut each sweet into three slices and place a piece in each hole. Make a small hole at the top of each tree.

3 Bake in the oven for 15-20 minutes, until the trees are golden and the sweets have melted, filling the holes. Cool on the baking sheets for five minutes and then transfer to a wire rack to cool. Thread lengths of ribbon through the holes at the top for hanging. Store in an airtight container until ready to hang.

Twiggy Stars

These pretty stars will look effective either hanging from the branches of the tree or displayed on the top.

YOU WILL NEED
secateurs (pruning shears)
willow twigs
stranded embroidery thread (floss)
scissors
checked cotton fabric
natural (garden) raffia (optional)

<u>**1**</u> For a large star to top the tree, cut the twigs into lengths of 15 cm (6 in) using the secateurs. For smaller stars to hang from the branches of the Christmas tree, cut the twigs into lengths of 5 cm (2 in). You will need five twigs for each star.

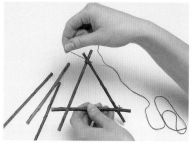

<u>**2**</u> Tie the first pair of twigs together near the ends with a length of embroidery thread, winding it around to form a 'V' shape. Repeat with the remaining twigs, arranging them under and over each other to form a five-pointed star.

<u>**3**</u> Cut the checked cotton fabric into thin strips approximately 15 x 2 cm (6 x ¾ in). Leave the ends frayed – this will add to the rustic look.

<u>**4**</u> Tie a length of fabric in a double knot over the thread at each point of the star. Attach a loop of raffia if the stars are to be hung.

BEADED FINIALS

These delicate creations, enhanced with pendant beads, started life as the cardboard backing on envelopes.

YOU WILL NEED
tracing paper
pencil
medium-weight manila cardboard
scissors
craft knife
metal ruler
cutting mat
bradawl
beads
flat-headed pins
long-nosed pliers
thin cord

1 Trace the templates from the back of the book. Transfer to cardboard twice and cut out. Mark the slotting slits down the centre of both pieces and cut out using a craft knife, metal ruler and cutting mat.

2 Make six small holes with a bradawl: one close to the bottom edge of one piece and one on the outside edge of the four top curls for inserting the beads, and a hole at the top for the hanging loop.

3 Thread the beads on to the pins. Bend each pin close to the top of the beads with pliers. Then hook the pins through the card. Wrap the ends around the pin, to secure.

4 After firmly slotting the two beaded card pieces together, thread a piece of cord through the top hole. Tie the ends to make a loop for hanging.

Indian-style Decorations

These bright salt dough ornaments evoke the vivid colours of an Indian festival.

You will need
two cups plain flour
one cup salt
one cup tepid water
large mixing bowl
wooden spoon
rolling pin
baking paper (parchment)
tracing paper
pencil
thin cardboard
scissors
sharp knife
cocktail stick (toothpick)
or drinking straw
baking sheet
medium and fine artist's paintbrushes
acrylic gesso
paints in bright colours
strong glue
selection of beads and sequins
matt acrylic varnish
thin ribbon

1 Mix the flour, salt and half the water, then gradually add more water. Knead for 10 minutes. Roll out the dough on baking paper. Trace the templates from the back of the book and cut out of the dough.

2 Dust the dough with flour. Make the patterns and detail in the dough using the point of a knife or a cocktail stick or drinking straw. Make a hole in the top of each shape for hanging. Moisten the ornaments.

3 Make smaller templates for the relief designs, cut out in dough and stick them to the figures. Place on a baking sheet and bake at 120°C/250°F/Gas 1 for 5 hours. Cool.

4 Prime with acrylic gesso. Leave to dry, then paint in bright colours. Glue on beads or sequins. Coat with acrylic varnish when dry. Thread the ribbon through the hole to hang.

SPARKLING STARS

Shimmering sequins and tiny beads make these hanging stars really shine.

YOU WILL NEED
polystyrene (styrofoam) star with
hanging loop
gold spray paint
small piece of plasticine
brown paper
multicoloured glass seed beads
multicoloured sequins
seed pearl beads
special design sequins
1.5 cm (⅝ in) brass-beaded pins
thin gold braid
scissors

1 Spray the polystyrene star with gold paint, anchoring it with a piece of plasticine to a sheet of brown paper to stop it moving. Allow to dry.

2 While the star is drying, sort the beads, sequins and pins into containers to make it easier to choose colours and shapes as you work.

3 Thread a glass seed bead on to a pin, followed by a multicoloured sequin. Push it gently into the star. Repeat to complete the design, covering the whole star. Pin a seed pearl bead and special design sequin in the centre of each side of the star.

4 For an alternative design, decorate the edges of the star with lines of sequins in contrasting colours. Pick out the "bones" of the star, in the same way, leaving the inner sections gold. Attach a length of gold braid though the loop to hang the star.

Glittering Cones

The intricate shape of these cones looks wonderful when highlighted with gold and sliver paint and glitter.

YOU WILL NEED
pine cones
red oxide spray primer
spray paints in gold and sliver
glue gun and glue sticks or all-purpose
glue and old fine paintbrush
assorted glitters
saucer
ribbon

1 To provide a good base colour for the spray paint, spray the cones with red oxide primer. Leave to dry for 1-2 hours. Ensure that all the recesses and details are well covered.

2 Spray the cones several times with gold or silver spray. Hold the can 25-30 cm (10-12 in) away from the cones as you spray, taking care to cover the whole cone. Leave to dry.

3 Heat up the glue gun and apply a little glue to the tips of each cone. Take care not to apply too much. Alternatively, apply small dabs of glue on to the cone tips with an old fine paintbrush.

4 Working quickly, sprinkle glitter on to the cones so that it sticks to the glued tips. Use a saucer to catch the excess glitter. When dry, glue a length of ribbon to the base of each cone for hanging.

APPLIQUED STARS

Mix and match these festive-coloured felt stars for a bold Christmas display.

YOU WILL NEED
tracing paper
soft pencil
thin cardboard
scissors
felt in red and green
tailor's chalk
embroidery scissors
needle
matching threads
ribbon
scraps of patterned fabric

1 Using the template at the back of the book, cut out the same number of red and green stars. Pierce some of the red stars 5 mm (¼ in) from the edge. Cut out smaller stars, leaving a 5 mm (¼ in) border all round.

2 Stitch a red border to one of the green stars with small, even running stitches. Centre a small red star on a green star and sew 5 mm (¼ in) from the edge again using small, neat running stitches.

3 Place these stars together, sandwiching a plain red star in the middle. Stitch the three stars together at the inner points. Sew a loop of ribbon to one of the points.

4 For a variation, cut a small circle in the centre of a green star. Place a piece of patterned fabric and a red star behind it. Stitch around the hole. Sew the edges of the stars together.

Heraldic Hangings

These stylish salt dough decorations look good enough to eat, but are purely ornamental.

YOU WILL NEED
two cups plain flour
one cup salt
one cup tepid water
large mixing bowl
wooden spoon
rolling pin
baking paper (parchment)
tracing paper
pencil
scissors
small, sharp knife
boiled sweets (hard candies)
cocktail stick (toothpick)
baking sheet
acrylic gesso
paintbrushes
gold craft paint
water-based satin varnish
jewels or sequins (optional)
glue (optional)
fine gold cord

Jewels, sequins and painted patterns enhance classic shapes such as fleur-de-lys and stars.

1 Mix flour, salt and water to a firm dough. Knead for 10 minutes. Roll the dough out flat on baking paper to a thickness of 5 mm (¼ in). Trace the templates at the back of the book and cut out of the dough. Dust with flour and place a sweet in the centre. Cut around the sweet, adding a 2 mm (⅛ in) margin.

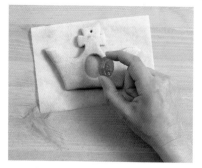

2 Make a hole for hanging in the top of each shape with a cocktail stick. Transfer the ornaments, without the sweets, on the paper to a baking sheet and bake at 120°C/250°F/Gas 1 for 9 hours. Place a boiled sweet in each hole and return to the oven for 30 minutes. Remove from the oven and set aside to cool.

3 Paint the shapes with gesso and allow to dry. Then paint them with gold paint and allow to dry overnight. Apply five coats of varnish, leaving to dry between applications. Jewels or sequins can also be added at this stage by gluing them on to the surface. Hang the ornaments from gold cord through the top hole.

Papier-Mache Decorations

These colourful ornaments are easy to make from scraps of newspaper.

You will need
tracing paper
pencil
thin cardboard
craft knife
cutting mat
small metal jewellery findings
strong clear glue
newspaper

diluted PVA (white) glue
container for glue
artist's paintbrushes
white paint
poster paints
paint-mixing palette
clear gloss varnish
thin cord

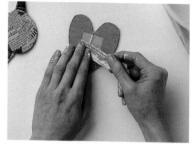

1 Cut cardboard templates from the back of the book and glue a jewellery finding on to the back of each ornament. Allow to dry, then cover with three layers of thin newspaper strips soaked in diluted PVA glue. Dry overnight and prime with a coat of white paint. Leave to dry.

2 Draw your design, then paint with poster paints. Seal with a coat of varnish and suspend with thin cord.

TEMPLATES

These templates can be scaled up or down on a photocopier as required.

Shiny Snowflakes pp 8–9

Wire Angel pp 16–17

Gilded Stars pp 20–21

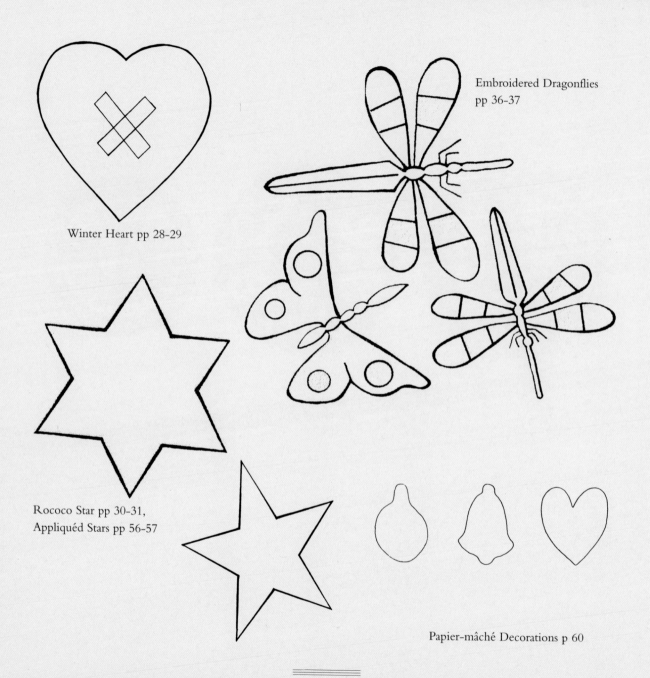

Winter Heart pp 28–29

Embroidered Dragonflies
pp 36–37

Rococo Star pp 30-31,
Appliquéd Stars pp 56-57

Papier-mâché Decorations p 60

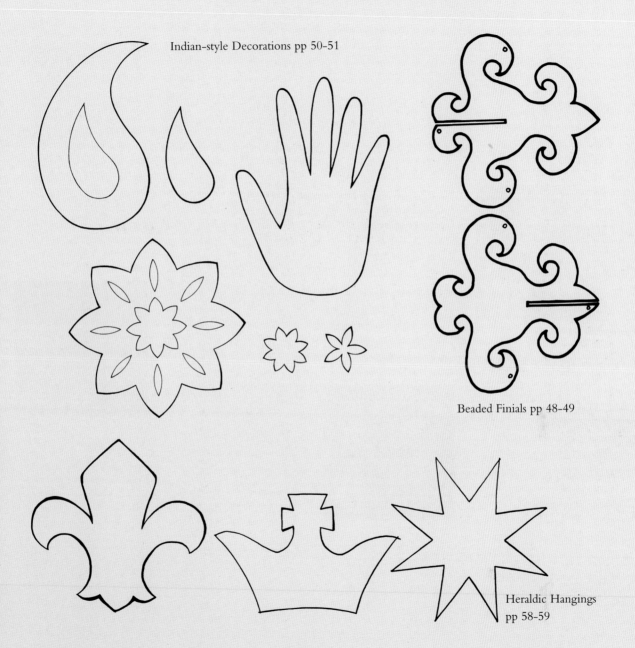

Indian-style Decorations pp 50-51

Beaded Finials pp 48-49

Heraldic Hangings
pp 58-59

INDEX

angel, wire, 16–17
appliquéd stars, 56–7

balls:
  gilded glass spheres, 42
  glittery balls, 15

  raffia balls, 14
  ribbon ornaments, 12–13
  sequinned balls, 10–11
beads:
  beaded finials, 48–9
  sequinned balls, 10–11
  sparkling stars, 52–3
biscuits, gilding, 23
button garland, 43

candles, 38
cinnamon sticks, 38
cone parcel, 12–13
cones, glittering, 54–5

dragonflies, embroidered, 36–7
dried fruit decorations, 26–7

edible ornaments, 44–5
eggs, harlequin, 18–19
embroidered dragonflies, 36–7

festive figures, 40
finials, beaded, 48–9
floral stars and trees, 26–7
fruit, 38
  dried fruit decorations, 26–7
  gilding, 23

garland, button, 43
gilded glass spheres, 42
gilded stars, 20–1
gilding, 23
gingerbread plaques, 24–5
glass spheres, gilded, 42
glittering cones, 54–5

glittery balls, 15
golden tassel, 12–13

hanging jugglers, 34–5
harlequin eggs, 18–19
heart, winter, 28–9
heraldic hangings, 58–9

Indian-style decorations, 50–1

jugglers, hanging, 34–5

mushrooms, gilding, 23

nuts, gilding, 23

oranges:
  classic pomanders, 39
  orange rings, 38

papier-mâché decorations, 60
plaques, gingerbread, 24–5
pomanders, classic, 39
precious shells, 22

raffia balls, 14
ribbon ornaments, 12–13
rococo star, 30–1

salt dough:
  heraldic hangings, 58–9
  Indian-style decorations, 50–1

sequins:
  sequinned balls, 10–11
  sparkling stars, 52–3
shells, precious, 22
snowflakes, shiny, 8–9
sparkling stars, 52–3
stars:
  appliquéd stars, 56–7
  floral stars, 26–7
  gilded stars, 20–1
  rococo star, 30–1
  sparkling stars, 52–3
  twiggy star, 46–7

tassels:
  elegant tassels, 32–3
  golden tassel, 12–13
templates, 61–3
twiggy star, 46–7

winter heart, 28–9
wire angel, 16–17